POSTCARD HISTORY SERIES

Chautauqua Institution

If you have not spent a week at Chautauqua you do not know your own country There and in no other place known to me, do you meet Baddeck and Newfoundland and Florida and Tiajuara at the same table and there you are of one heart and one soul with the forty thousand people who will drift in and out people all of them who believe in God and in their country

Edward Everett Hale, in Tarry at Home Travels."

COPYRIGHT, 1909 BY CHAUTAUQUA PRESS

Edward Everett Hale (1822–1909), author of the short story "The Man without a Country" and other well-known books, was a champion for popular education and for the Chautauqua Movement in particular. Hale's book *In His Name* (published in 1873) was a selected reading for the Chautauqua Literary and Scientific Circle (CLSC). In 1903, Hale became chaplain of the US Senate. When asked if he prayed for the senators he replied, "No, I look at the senators and I pray for the country." (Courtesy of the Chautauqua Institution Archives.)

ON THE FRONT COVER: Between lectures, performances, classes, and other scheduled activities, visitors always have the opportunity to enjoy a peaceful stroll along the shores of Chautauqua Lake. From morning mists to evening sunsets, the lake's ever-changing appearance provides a perfect setting for reflection away from the distractions of everyday life. (Courtesy of the Chautauqua Institution Archives.)

ON THE BACK COVER: For the first 40 years, most people arrived at the Chautauqua by steamboat after traveling to the lake by train. The Pier Building, the hotels, and the cottages along the shoreline provided an exciting welcome for visitors regardless of whether they were coming for the season, a week, or just a day. (Courtesy of the Chautauqua Institution Archives.)

POSTCARD HISTORY SERIES

Chautauqua Institution

Jonathan David Schmitz and William Flanders

ARCADIA
PUBLISHING

Published by Arcadia Publishing
Charleston, South Carolina

Printed in the United States of America

Library of Congress Control Number: 2010940118

For all general information contact Arcadia Publishing at:
Telephone 843-853-2070
Fax 843-853-0044
E-mail sales@arcadiapublishing.com
For customer service and orders:
Toll-Free 1-888-313-2665

Visit us on the Internet at www.arcadiapublishing.com

*To all the Chautauquans, past and present, who
have made Chautauqua what it is today.*

CONTENTS

ACKNOWLEDGMENTS

Most of the postcards in this volume belong to the Chautauqua Institution Archives and have been acquired over the years from a number of individuals. Recent donations by Syd Baker and Ron Moskowitz were particularly important in building this collection, which is now housed in the Oliver Archives Center. In addition, the following individuals have loaned or donated postcards for this book: Caroline Van Kirk Bissell, indicated by CVB; Joanne Fuller, indicated by JF; and William Flanders, indicated by WF. Special appreciation is owed to those who have volunteered their time at the archives and to Bill Flanders and Joan Smith, who have worked extensively on identifying and describing the thousands of postcards at the Oliver Archives Center and know them better than anyone. A word of thanks should be made to the archives staff, particularly Marlie Bendiksen and Jason Rodriguez, and to Noah Goodling who spent many hours scanning the images. And special thanks is also owed to the archivist's wife, Elizabeth Schmitz, for reading and correcting the text.

INTRODUCTION

Anyone who is familiar with Chautauqua knows the place is not easy to describe. Characteristically complex, Chautauqua brings together in one place and in one season as much as is possible. It embraces all subjects, all faiths, and all forms of art and recreation. Chautauqua integrates education, religion, the arts, and recreation into a shared experience that not only provides a good time, but also teaches a lesson in how to make good use of time.

Organized by John Vincent and Lewis Miller, the Chautauqua Institution started in 1874 as an outdoor summer retreat for Sunday school workers. But Chautauqua was more than just a Sunday school—it was about the Sabbath itself. According to Vincent, every day at Chautauqua was the Sabbath. Then and now, the Chautauqua season is an extended Sabbath of sorts—a special season in the year, just like Sunday is a special day in the week. During the weekdays, work and worry too often keep friends and family apart from one another and from what we really want to do. But on the Sabbath, we reassemble as a community to worship, to rest, and to reacquaint ourselves with our faith. And so it is at Chautauqua. But Chautauqua was not born from the imagination of one or even two individuals. It was, and still is, the product of many hearts and minds. Sometimes the lofty ideas worked together; at other times they worked at odds, producing a place and a program beyond what any individual could conceive. Chautauqua succeeded because it met a need shared by Americans across the country, and it thrives today for the same reason.

The Chautauqua Movement brought together three American institutions of the 19th century. The use of an outdoor venue was taken from the camp meetings of the time. Lifelong learning and self-improvement came from the lyceum movement while the Sunday school movement provided for Chautauqua's purpose and mission. All three institutions were in decline after the Civil War, but John Vincent managed to use the appeal of each to address the weaknesses of the others to create the Chautauqua movement. As James A. Garfield said, "It has been the struggle of the world to get more leisure, but it was left to Chautauqua to show how to use it."

And leisure was not to be wasted, at least not at Chautauqua. It was to be used well. In the early years, vice and questionable amusements, such as card playing and dancing, were not permitted at Chautauqua—even smoking was discouraged, and, of course, alcohol was absolutely forbidden. These rules were gradually relaxed over the years, but they were important for Chautauqua's early success. They helped to make Chautauqua a place that was safe, particularly for women and children, and this safety gave women and children more freedom than they typically would enjoy throughout the rest of the year. This safety, combined with a healthy climate, clean water, and the unexplained absence of disease-carrying mosquitoes, allowed fathers to feel comfortable leaving their families at Chautauqua during the week, while they returned to their jobs in the cities (or indulged in the vices prohibited at Chautauqua—and by their wives when they were at home).

So what did visitors do? For Chautauquans, there is no better use of time than time spent learning. For Vincent, all subjects and creation were worthy of study. "To Chautauquans, all things hold a measure of God's wisdom," he wrote. "Things secular are under God's governance, and are full of divine meanings. If God created all things, if he governs all things, if the channels of history have been furrowed by his own hand, if the beating life of the physical universe is from him who is Life before life, Life of all life, then nothing is secular in any sense as to make it foreign or unattractive to the saints of God."

But the founders knew that not all learning was education—education required structure. So, to provide a structure for lifelong learning, Vincent announced at the fifth Chautauqua Assembly in 1878 the beginning of a four-year reading course designed to provide those unable to attend college the opportunity to acquire the basic knowledge and skills of a college graduate by reading in their spare time. The program was called the Chautauqua Literary and Scientific Circle (CLSC). The response exceeded expectation and the program rapidly grew through the last decades of the 19th century reaching tens of thousands of students who were unable to acquire an education because they were too busy, too poor, or lived too far away.

With the popularity of the CLSC, a number of new, similar organizations known as "daughter Chautauquas" formed and spread Chautauqua to other parts of the country. The over 250 daughter Chautauquas that formed during the 19th century have spread the Chautauqua name across the continent and beyond. Daughter Chautauquas were essentially autonomous and only loosely affiliated with the original mother Chautauqua in New York. Talent agents in New York, Boston, Philadelphia, and Chicago supplied the speakers and entertainers for these platforms and coined the term "Chautauqua talent" to describe a form of entertainment that was not only safe (meaning it met moral standards similar to vaudeville) but was actually good for audiences because it was edifying and educational. Eventually, the demand for this entertainment led talent agents to put Chautauqua programs on the road. Known as "traveling Chautauquas," "tent Chautauquas," or "circuit Chautauquas," these shows were privately owned and had no contractual or administrative connection with Chautauqua, but they spread the name and the movement to its furthest limits, reaching millions of Americans and Canadians in the early decades of the 20th century.

The original Chautauqua and some others are still open for visitors today. Guests come from all over the country to see the place Theodore Roosevelt described as "typically American in that it is typical of America at its best." A visit to the Chautauqua of the past is contained within the pages of this book. Chautauqua's history has been intimately preserved in images sent by visitors to families and friends by way of postcards.

One

"Dear Friends: This is Chautauqua . . ."

People often learn about a place from postcards with the usual friendly message scrawled on the back: "I am having a wonderful time and wish you were here." Today, such brief messages are relayed with a text message, a Facebook post, or a tweet on Twitter. In contrast, postcards provide an enduring image as seen through the photographer's eyes from a century past.

This first group of postcards from Chautauqua introduces this distinctive place as if the reader had received these cards from a friend. Readers will be transported back in time to explore Chautauqua at various points in its history. In subsequent chapters, readers will continue to see and learn more about Chautauqua and all it had to offer.

JOHN H. VINCENT AND LEWIS MILLER
FOUNDERS OF CHAUTAUQUA INSTITUTION
CHAUTAUQUA, N. Y.

John Vincent (left) and Lewis Miller had much in common. They were close in age; both were from modest backgrounds; neither ever attended college; and both were successful. Most of all, both were religious men who believed in education and thought it impossible to understand religious truth so long as it remained set apart from a general understanding of the world. Together in 1874, they set about creating a two-week program to train and educate Sunday school teachers. The program combined science, literature, the arts, and recreation with the study and practice of religion. The 25-year friendship of Vincent and Miller was the start of the Chautauqua community.

BISHOP JOHN H. VINCENT

Chancellor Emeritus of Chautauqua Institution

"SELF-IMPROVEMENT in all our faculties,
for all of us, through all time, for the greatest
good of all people—this is the Chautauqua idea,
a divine idea, a democratic idea, a progressive
idea, a millennial idea."

John Vincent (1832–1920) was born in Tuscaloosa, Alabama, but moved north at a young age. He became licensed to preach in the Methodist Episcopal church in 1849 and served as a circuit rider in New Jersey, Ohio, and Illinois. Prior to the Civil War, Vincent was a pastor in Galena, Illinois, where the yet unknown Ulysses S. Grant was a parishioner. (President Grant would come to see Chautauqua for himself in its second year.) In 1866, Vincent was appointed a general agent of the Methodist Sunday School Union. In 1873, he asked Lewis Miller to host a two-week program in Akron, Ohio, to teach Sunday school workers the new curriculum. Instead, the two men began plans for a national Sunday school assembly to be held at Fair Point on Chautauqua Lake the following year.

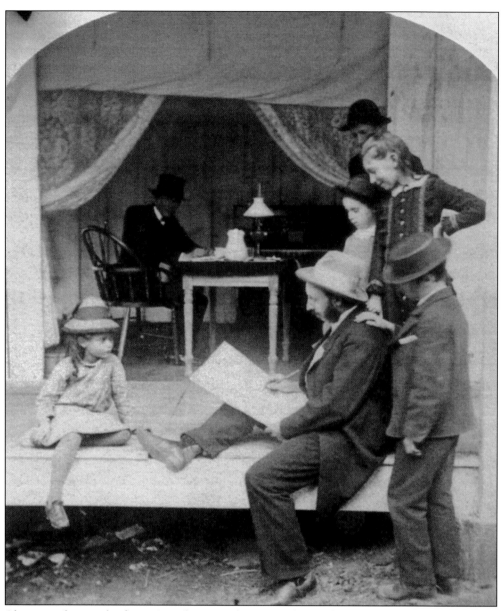

Always ready to poke fun at just about anything, Frank Beard (1842–1905) entertained early Chautauqua assemblies as a "chalk talk" artist. Using just a few strokes, Beard could transform a drawing from one thing to another as part of a humorous monologue with a moral lesson attached. He enchanted Chautauqua audiences with his sketches and general humor both on and off the stage. He is shown here sitting on the porch of "Knowers' Ark," a crude lakeside guesthouse for assembly lecturers and performers. An unidentified lecturer is seated inside preparing his talk. Beard exhibits a more artistic temperament in his appearance in contrast to the other lecturer's dress. Note the day-curtains and the heavy canvas that could be rolled down against the night chill. Though this was a camping experience, even children were well dressed. Beard performed at many of the daughter Chautauquas and was an active supporter of the Chautauqua Movement. In later years, he became a Christian magazine editor and cartoonist of great influence.

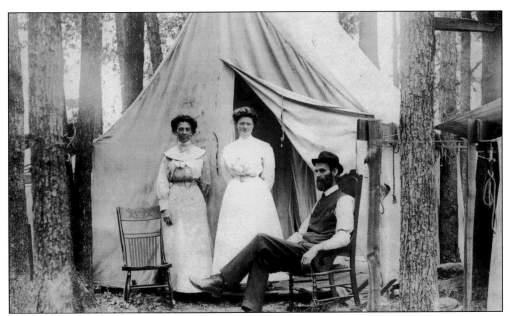

During the first Chautauqua Assembly, most people stayed in tents. There were more than 100 small tents encircling the outdoor auditorium at the first assembly. Meals served in the dining tent cost 50¢, and straw for bedding was furnished at no charge. Tent platforms were used as floors for the first cottages that followed the early camping experience. Today, there are still cottages that retain the dimensions of those early tent platforms.

MILLER COTTAGE, SUMMER HOME OF THOMAS A. EDISON, CHAUTAUQUA INSTITUTION   CHAUTAUQUA, N. Y.

The materials for Lewis Miller's cottage were pre-cut in and shipped from Akron, Ohio, for quick assembly at Chautauqua. An ornate tent stood at the right of the cottage for extra sleeping space. Miller's daughter Mina married Thomas Edison, whose friends Henry Ford and Harvey Firestone were often guests at the cottage.

This street scene from 1906 shows the Administration Building on the left (now restored as the Hultquist Center). The Chautauqua Amphitheater is in the background. The building on the right served as the museum and was known as Newton Hall. It stood on the corner that is now occupied by the Smith Memorial Library. An Egyptian mummy and a statue from an Egyptian tomb were among some of the many exhibits found in the museum.

This postcard shows the same street pictured above with the addition of a brick walk leading to the Chautauqua Amphitheater. The building on the right served as a museum and housed the information office. The structure with the columns and porches served as the CLSC building and housed a bookstore. The small booth standing just beyond the CLSC building is located near the site of the present-day gazebo.

This 1898 view of Chautauqua's Chautauqua Amphitheater stage and audience is half of a double postcard designed to be separated into two cards. These cards were used for advertising. Notice that the misspelled name has been crossed out and corrected. Ahlstrom pianos were manufactured in Jamestown, New York, from 1900 to 1926. C.A. Ahlstrom developed the tone system controlled by the left pedal on most upright pianos today. (Courtesy of CVB.)

Audiences filled the hard Chautauqua Amphitheater benches to hear renowned speakers from across the country. The distinguished man in the lower right corner with the pince-nez glasses was not part of the original photograph.

Choral arrangements with orchestral accompaniments were regularly performed at Chautauqua. Seated in front of the orchestra are, among others, Horatio Cornell, head of the voice department; Sol Marcosson, violin instructor; Alfred Hallam, supervisor of music; and Arthur Bestor, president of the Chautauqua Institution. Henry Vincent, organist and nephew of John Vincent, is standing in front of the organ console with his hand on his hip.

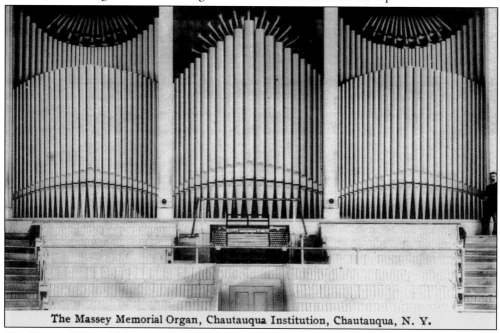

The Massey Memorial Organ, Chautauqua Institution, Chautauqua, N. Y.

The Massey Memorial Organ, a gift to Chautauqua from the Hart Massey Foundation in 1907, remains the largest outdoor organ in the world. Hart Massey (1823–1896) was a manufacturer of farm implements and a friend of Lewis Miller. Massey served as a trustee for the Chautauqua Assembly. Massey's son Chester (who married John Vincent's sister) also served as a trustee, as did Massey's grandson Vincent (who went on to become the first Canadian ambassador to the United States and first Canadian governor general of Canada). Another of Massey's grandsons, actor Raymond Massey, wrote that his first exposure to theater was at Chautauqua.

As the popularity of Chautauqua spread, new buildings were erected to house growing audiences. The most notable of these were the Chautauqua Amphitheater and the original Hall of Philosophy, both built in 1879. In this view, cofounder John Vincent is seen standing in front of the Hall of Philosophy.

The visitors pictured in this postcard from 1907 must have been impressed by the new Hall of Philosophy. Designed by the Buffalo, New York, architect Edward R. Green, it replaced the previous Hall of Philosophy, which was built in 1879. The plank walkway indicates that this view was taken prior to the completion of the building. The torches on cement pedestals, described by the *Chautauquan Daily* as "Athenian watch fires," are also not yet in place.

A fire destroyed several wooden buildings located in the center of what is today Bestor Memorial Plaza. Kellogg Hall and other buildings were moved from this site in 1905 to open the space in front of the newly constructed Colonnade Building and make the plaza the center of the Chautauqua grounds. The Colonnade housed the administrative offices, stores, and the printing shop. The printing shop was moved to the new post office building after 1909.

The Vine Clad Pergola, Chautauqua Institution, Chautauqua, N. Y.

The first Colonnade Building (left) included shops and had a balcony with a curved staircase. At one time, tea and refreshments were served on the balcony as patrons relaxed and surveyed the activity on the plaza below. The Pergola served as an open marketplace for dairy products and other items.

529 The Ruined Colonnade, Chautauqua N.Y.
After the Fire Oct. 19, 1908

The Colonnade Building burned twice: once in 1908 and again in 1961. The first building was destroyed just three years after its construction in 1905. Some of the walls and the columns were used in the rebuilding. Fires have always been a great concern at Chautauqua, and Chautauquans considered themselves fortunate that these fires did not spread to the wooden structures nearby.

Today, the volunteer fire department provides ambulance service with trained EMTs and fire protection. With its modern equipment, wireless communications, and mutual aid from adjacent fire companies, Chautauqua has come a long way since these uniformed firefighters posed for this photograph in 1909.

THE COLONNADE, CHAUTAUQUA INSTITUTION, CHAUTAUQUA, N. Y.

After it burned in the fire of 1908, the Colonnade Building was rebuilt and ready for the next season in 1909. A third floor with dormers was added for use as rental apartments. In the winter of 1961, a tenant's heater may have been the cause of the second Colonnade fire. The temperature dipped to nearly zero degrees that day, and ice coated both the building and the firemen. The fire claimed the life of one female tenant who went back into the building to retrieve her belongings. A third Colonnade Building was constructed after the fire in 1961.

New Post Office, Chautauqua, N. Y.

There was much activity on the plaza in 1909 with the construction of the new Colonnade Building and the post office. The architectural firm of Green and Wicks was exceptionally busy as the first section of the Arts and Crafts Quadrangle was also built that year. The new post office housed the print shop in the basement, which was later used for the bookstore.

The Administration Building was used for a variety of purposes after the colonnade was built in 1905, but it is best remembered for the Oriental bazaar run by the Rashid family in the 1930s. Rebuilt in 1999 as the Hultquist Center, the building's exterior appearance is similar to the original structure of 1889, but it now houses modern meeting facilities.

The CLSC's home reading studies program brought national recognition to Chautauqua, drawing many visitors who came to experience Chautauqua firsthand. The imposing CLSC building, which stood alongside the walkway to the Chautauqua Amphitheater, was where students could enroll in the reading course (with the help of secretary Kate Kimball) and buy that year's CLSC books.

Ada May Smith-Wilkes donated the money to build the Smith Memorial Library in 1931 in honor of her parents. Chautauqua finally had a library in keeping with the rest of its facilities. It remains open all year and is part of a two-county library system. It is a favorite meeting place for the community in both summer and winter. The museum and CLSC buildings were razed for the library's construction.

Chautauqua has always drawn capacity crowds for its summer programs. An evening performance attracts thousands whether it is for a symphony concert, a ballet, a lecture from a well-known scholar or lawmaker, or a rock-and-roll band. The Chautauqua Amphitheater was built in a natural ravine and has excellent acoustics, a feature that was particularly important before the era of electronics.

Norton Hall was under construction when Franklin D. Roosevelt, then governor of New York, came to Chautauqua on July 13, 1929, with his wife, Eleanor, and his son, Elliot. Ralph Norton and Chautauqua president Arthur Bestor were waiting to greet them. All three members of the Roosevelt family returned to Chautauqua to speak at different times. The most remembered appearance was in 1936 when President Roosevelt delivered his "I Hate War" speech in the Chautauqua Amphitheater.

In her book, *Chautauqua Salute, A Memoir of the Bestor Years*, Mary Frances Cram (daughter of Arthur Bestor) remembers standing in the hallway of her home at Chautauqua holding the text of a speech for Eleanor Roosevelt while the first lady discussed on the telephone with her husband in Washington what she would say in the Chautauqua Amphitheater. Later, FDR himself would be entertained here, as were Amelia Earhart and a number of nationally known speakers.

Over the years, Chautauquans have spent many warm summer afternoons relaxing inside this open-air Grecian temple or outside on its benches. Lectures on a wide range of subjects occurred here. Today, this more intimate venue has become so popular that the audience brings chairs and fills much of the lawn space beyond the hall. The talks and discussions are amplified by a sound system.

In the afternoon, the Hall of Philosophy is the site of a variety of lectures by religious leaders of all faiths. The lectures are sponsored by the Department of Religion and included programs of national interest by the Women's Club and appearances by authors of the current CLSC book selections. The floor of this building has tile mosaics representing the graduating classes of the CLSC.

The symphony concerts in the Chautauqua Amphitheater have always been an important feature of the Chautauqua season. Starting in 1923, the New York Symphony took up summer residence at Chautauqua, and in 1929, the Chautauqua Symphony Orchestra was formed with Albert Stoessel appointed the first music director. Today, the symphony consists of accomplished musicians from orchestras around the world

Norton Hall, a gift from Ralph Norton's wife in memory of her husband and daughter, was built in 1929. This Art Deco monolithic concrete structure provided an indoor facility for opera and theater. Today, theatrical performances are held next door in the Bratton Theater. With the support of the Chautauqua Opera Guild and Friends of the Theater, both art forms have become essential to the Chautauqua summer.

Normal Hall, Chautauqua Institution, Chautauqua, New York.

Normal Hall was built in 1885 and is one of the oldest buildings on the Chautauqua grounds. In 2000, it was thoroughly renovated and rededicated as Bratton Theater in honor of Dan Bratton, president of the Chautauqua Institution from 1984 to 2000. The building is now a state-of-the-art facility used by the Chautauqua Theater Company.

443. Chautauqua Lake, N. Y. Cottages at Chautauqua.

Chautauqua has religion, lectures, music, theater, dance, art, and recreation, and it also offers a community with limited automobile traffic. It is a place for walking and discovering charming cottages and scenes as one explores the avenues named after people who were instrumental in developing Chautauqua.

Two

"Dear Friends: Our Trip Here . . ."

Consider for a moment what it was like to get around in the age of steam. Travelers needed to check train schedules, compare prices, and see if an excursion rate was being offered. They would probably need to change trains at some point or even stay overnight in Buffalo, Chicago, or Pittsburgh. Travelers could take their time traveling if they had time to spare. It was simple enough to get off a train for a visit or a side-trip and then simply continue on to the next train. Food could be purchased at most stops along the way, and some travelers made good use of the dining car with its spotless linen and excellent service.

After arriving at the Mayville train station, travelers needed to cross the tracks to the large dock to purchase a ticket for the next steamboat ride across the lake. Hopefully, their trunks were not far behind. Once those traveling to Chautauqua made it aboard the boat, the whistle would sound and the steamboat would start down the lake. From the starboard side of the boat, travelers could see cottages between trees on the shoreline. From the port side of the boat, there were other steamboats on the lake carrying passengers and several fishing boats catching muskellunge or "muskies" to sell to the restaurants and resorts around the lake. After disembarking at the Pier Building, visitors first needed to buy a gate pass. Gate passes were good for a day, a week, or for the whole season. Guests had to be careful not to lose the pass because they needed the pass not just to enter the grounds, but to leave as well. If a guest tried to leave without it, they would be charged for the entire season. Once Chautauqua guests got their gate pass, they could begin looking for their luggage.

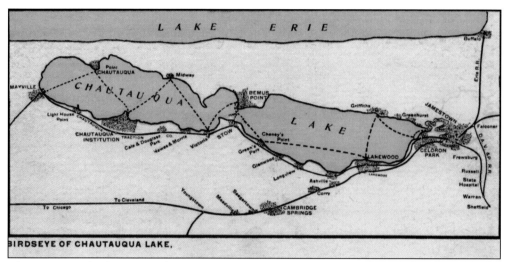

BIRDSEYE OF CHAUTAUQUA LAKE,

Chautauqua Lake lies on a plateau above Lake Erie in western New York. By the 1880s, the lake had become a popular summer resort location with large hotels along its shores. Railroads promoted vacations to Chautauqua Lake by offering excursion fares. Steamboats carried passengers to destinations along the lake, and later, trolley lines on both shores made connections by land.

Chautauqua, N. Y.

The idea of learning and having fun at the same time in a lovely setting has attracted thousands of visitors to Chautauqua in past summers just as it still does today. Postcards showing the lake and Chautauqua were used to increase interest in the area. This postcard shows a detailed pen-and-ink drawing of Chautauqua in the early 1900s. The drawing is so detailed that even some of the buildings are recognizable.

In the early days, travelers could take the train to Mayville, New York, on the Buffalo, Corry & Pittsburgh Railroad (later the Pennsylvania Railroad). A sleeper car would arrive from Pittsburgh during the night to be placed on a short railroad track known as a siding. In the morning after a good breakfast, the passengers could embark on a steamboat to Chautauqua or other resorts down the lake.

By 1907, the Pennsylvania Railroad Company built a substantial steamboat dock to facilitate the transfer of passengers to the steamboats. The Mayville waterfront was a busy place in those days with hotels and restaurants nearby to handle all the people arriving at or departing from Chautauqua and other points along the lake.

In 1912, steamboats offered the best means of travel from Mayville to Chautauqua. One such boat was the *City of Cleveland*, shown here with its pilothouse surmounted by an eagle. A poster on the steamboat's bow advertises Celeron Park, an amusement park, and its vaudeville acts. Celeron Park was created on the southern part of the lake to increase revenue for the Jamestown Street Railway Company and for the steamboat operators.

Steamboats both large and small were the primary means of transportation on the lake, and there was a strong competition for passengers. By 1914, the Broadhead family of Jamestown had acquired most of the steamboats and the trolley lines on both sides of the lake. Just 10 years later, the automobile made this transportation network nearly obsolete.

The steamboats from Mayville or Jamestown arrived at Chautauqua at the Pier Building, which was built in 1886. The rapid growth of Chautauqua's attendance created an expansion of the steamboat fleet. From 1875 to 1880, eight more steamboats were built at sites along the lake. In the horse-and-buggy era, steamers provided a fast and comfortable means of getting to lakeside destinations.

This is the Pier Building at Chautauqua with the *City of Chicago* as seen from the deck of another steamboat. No steamboats were allowed to dock on Sunday. The decorum of the Sabbath was not to be disturbed by crowds arriving on their only day of leisure. Today, no admission is charged on Sunday and many people come to services and other Chautauqua events on that day.

Landing at Chautauqua was not always without problems. On August 8, 1908, the *City of Cincinnati* struck a submerged pile and sank at the pier. A gangplank from the bow enabled the passengers to leave safely. The steamer was refloated and repaired and remained a favorite boat on the lake for another 19 years. The small steamboat *City of Rochester* is shown standing by.

Visitors to Chautauqua were able to take one of the many boats to Jamestown, Celeron Park, or Midway for amusements, or to the resort hotels at Lakewood and Bemus Point. Those who were so inclined were able to escape Chautauqua's prohibition of alcohol by taking a steamboat to another part of the lake and letting the pilot do the driving.

An even faster means of travel arrived at Chautauqua on July 4, 1904. The Chautauqua Traction Company line served the west side of the lake from Jamestown. It expanded to serve Westfield by 1909. Some of the open cars serving Chautauqua could hold 80 passengers and reach a speed of 50 miles per hour. Candles were provided in case of a power failure.

The New Traction Station, Chautauqua Institution,   Chautauqua, N. Y.

When the trolley line became the most important means of getting to Chautauqua from Jamestown, Lakewood, and Mayville, Chautauqua moved the main gate to its present location. The new gate was more impressive than the earlier gates and better designed to handle automobile traffic. The architect firm of Green and Wicks of Buffalo, New York, used rows of columns in the main gate just as they did for other buildings at Chautauqua.

By 1926, the trolleys no longer went to Chautauqua and the automobile was now the primary means of transportation. The roads leading to Chautauqua were just being paved at that time. Visitors knew they were at Chautauqua when they drove onto the brick pavement that stretched the length of the grounds.

Since automobile use within the grounds was restricted, a large building across from the main gate was used for parking. The structure was formerly used as a livery stable. In August 1922, a fire completely demolished this building and all of the cars stored within. Fortunately, many cars were parked along the fence and escaped damage.

After trolley services stopped, those without cars relied on busses. The West Ridge Bus Company provided frequent service from Jamestown to Westfield and stopped at Chautauqua on the way. For those arriving in cars, temporary parking was allowed while people bought their tickets, but cars were then required to park along the fence or elsewhere. Today, there are several large parking lots outside the gate.

A large steel arch spanning the width of the road marked the entrance to Chautauqua. Written across the top of the building to the left was the motto, "Chautauqua—Where Education and Recreation Meet in a Delightful Summer Colony," to remind visitors why they had come. Today, this building houses the ticket windows and serves as an information center for the institution and the region in general. The actual entrance gate is located beyond the building.

Arriving at Chautauqua by seaplane would have been convenient. In 1914, Chautauqua actually had daily service by a Curtis seaplane, but it was only allowed to carry postcards and an occasional daring passenger. The Bumble Bee was flown by A.J. Engel from its base at Celeron Park. This plane is on permanent display at the Crawford Museum in Cleveland, Ohio.

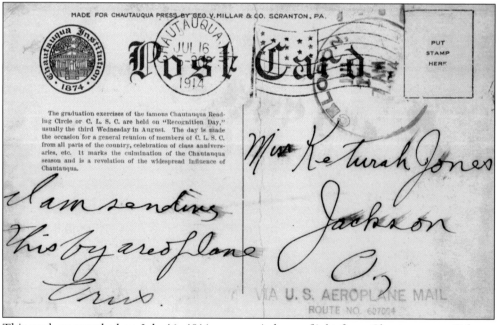

This card, postmarked on July 16, 1914, was carried on a flight from Chautauqua to Celeron "by aeroplane." Postcards were allowed to be carried on flights in 1914 only by special permit as a publicity measure. Regular airmail began with US Army pilots in 1918. Private airlines took over in 1921. (Courtesy of W.F.)

Three

"DEAR FRIENDS: OUR FIRST DAY HERE . . ."

Take a walk through Chautauqua using the route indicated by these postcards as a guide. Try to locate the places where the photographer stood to take the pictures. Many of the places are not very different today, but some postcards may require a careful scanning to find one or two details that still exist. In some locations, there are plaques describing the previous buildings.

Most of these postcards show images of Chautauqua from 1906 to 1919. Fortunately, postcards were enough of a novelty that they were saved and collected. Their size was just right to fit into a shoebox and some even made it into albums. With the advent of computers and digital cameras, photo albums may soon be a thing of the past.

After showing their tickets and entering through the gate, visitors would see a long brick street leading toward the center of Chautauqua. The knobbed posts prevented vehicles from driving on the street (but could be pulled up to allow access to emergency vehicles). Chautauqua is a community designed for walking, although bicycles are popular as well.

The St. Elmo Hotel stood on the left side of Vincent Avenue as visitors approached the edge of the plaza. This hotel was very popular and remained open through the winter. Some retirees lived there year-round. The building is now the St. Elmo Condominium.

The plaza was named Bestor Memorial Plaza in 1946 to honor Arthur Bestor, Chautauqua's president from 1915 until his death in 1944. Chautauqua saw much change during these years, including two wars and the Great Depression, which nearly destroyed the institution. The flag in this picture stands where the fountain is today.

The Colonnade and Pergola
Chautauqua, N. Y., on Lake Chautauqua

This is how the Colonnade Building looked in the early 1930s. The Pergola was torn down in 1946. It had provided a marketplace to supplement the grocery store and meat market in the Colonnade Building. Also shown is Pratt Avenue, which ended at Vincent Avenue and became a walking path.

At the Book Store
Chautauqua Institution, Chautauqua, N. Y.

The post office and bookstore have not changed much since the 1920s when this picture was taken. A book sale appears to be in progress in front of a second entrance to the store. This entrance now holds an elevator for the store and post office. With the redesign of Bestor Memorial Plaza, the fountain sculpture from Norton Hall was relocated to stand in front of this building.

St. Elmo   Colonnade
The Plaza   Chautauqua Institution
Chautauqua, N. Y.

In the 1920s, there was no fountain in the center of the plaza as there is today, and the Florida Fountain, with its columns and tile roof, was in a different location. But the benches were occupied as people stopped to meet and chat just as today. Not much has really changed in the ambience that makes Chautauqua so recognizable.

The brick walk from the Chautauqua Amphitheater through the plaza was actually a street before the post office was built in 1909 and is still named Clark Street. There was a Western Union office in the post office building through the 1940s, and telegrams were delivered in the summer by the Western Union boy.

This scene from 1907 provides a glimpse into the past. An impatient man is leaning on his cane and holding his watch. The bicycle in the background indicates its growing popularity here. Cycling lessons were given at Chautauqua's bicycle club, and bloomers were becoming fashionable for female cyclists.

The Book Store, Chautauqua Institution Chautauqua, N. Y.

The sign on the awning announces the CLSC's British American Year. The CLSC building housed the bookstore before it was moved to the basement of the post office building. The bookstore published many of the Chautauqua postcards, as did the Chautauqua Press before it.

A Chautauqua scene from the 1930s looks much like today, except for the clothing. Boys wore knickers until they were in their teens, at which time they were allowed to wear long pants. A fence and gates at the Chautauqua Amphitheater can be seen in this picture. The use of walls and gates was reintroduced when the Chautauqua Amphitheater was renovated in the 1980s.

42

History of Chautauqua Institution

Founded in 1874, Chautauqua Institution is a community on the shores of Chautauqua Lake in southwestern New York state that comes alive each summer with a mix of lectures, fine and performing arts, interfaith worship, and recreational activities.

The first season at Chautauqua was held on the shoreline site still used today. Called the Chautauqua Lake Sunday School Assembly, it was a two-week, outdoor normal school for Sunday School workers. Chautauqua was to be an international affair, bringing visitors from across the United States and Canada to one place to hear the very best speakers on the Bible, Bible history, teaching methods, science and current social issues.

From the start, Chautauqua was about the right use of leisure time, lifelong learning and self-improvement through healthy recreation, guided study and worship — purposes that co-founder John Vincent referred to as "all about the Sabbath." The program proved immensely popular, and a second season was planned even before the first had finished.

As many as 20,000 people came the first season, but Chautauqua reached many more who had never even entered its gates. By teaching teachers, Chautauqua reached the whole nation; it was the first institution to give a certificate in physical education and one of the first to train music, pre-school and manual and fine arts teachers.

At the end of the fifth season, in 1878, John Vincent announced a year-round correspondence reading program, to be called the Chautauqua Literary and Scientific Circle, or simply the CLSC. It was open to all people of any age, sex, religion or race. The four-year course of study was to allow people who were unable to attend college to continue their education.

To keep interest and share the cost of books, CLSC students were encouraged to form reading circles in their communities, and these circles created their own chautauqua-like programs. At one time or another, there

(over)

were more than 250 such "Daughter Chautauquas" in the United States and Canada, some of which still exist today.

Starting in 1904, agents who provided the speakers and entertainers for such programs began to produce their own traveling chautauquas, also known as circuit or tent chautauquas, reaching millions of Americans and Canadians. Over time, however, high schools, universities and summer schools, as well as libraries, movies and radio, met many of the needs Chautauqua had addressed. This cultural evolution brought about the decline of the movement, while the Great Depression closed most of the remaining Daughter Chautauquas. Even Chautauqua Institution itself went into receivership. But through the efforts of the community, it bought back its debt in 1936.

Music became increasingly important at Chautauqua — especially after the turn of the century. A symphony orchestra season became part of the regular program in 1920. The Chautauqua Symphony Orchestra and the Chautauqua Opera Company, founded in 1929, continue to perform for Chautauqua audiences today. The Institution also is home to Chautauqua Theater Company, the Chautauqua Dance program, visual arts galleries and pre-professional Schools of Fine and Performing Arts.

The Chautauqua platform has established itself as a national forum for open discussions of public issues, international relations, literature and science, with such notable speakers through the years as Alexander Graham Bell, Franklin Delano Roosevelt, Margaret Mead, Thurgood Marshall and Elie Wiesel.

Chautauqua participants continue to gather each summer to reacquaint themselves with one another, to meet and welcome new members and to experience the same broad and diversified program that is at the heart of Chautauqua's community, identity and history.

—Jonathan Schmitz,
Chautauqua archivist and historian

Chautauqua Institution
PO Box 28
Chautauqua, NY 14722
chq.org

Rose Cottage, Chautauqua Institution   Chautauqua, N. Y.

Cottages at Chautauqua retain much of their early charm. After World War II, land was made available for new housing on the north end, and today, nearly every form of architectural style can be found on the grounds. Since the 1980s on, there has been a demand for modern improvements, and like this cottage, some structures have been tastefully restored.

Summer Homes
Chautauqua Institution
Chautauqua, N. Y.

The cottages and rooming houses in the old section of Chautauqua were built on lots of only 40 by 50 feet, making multistoried structures necessary. These multilevel porches allowed guests to take meals outside, entertain friends, relax with a book, or simply enjoy the view. The proximity of these buildings to one another was done deliberately to promote a closer sense of community.

The brick walk winds around the Chautauqua Amphitheater and continues to Smith-Wilkes Hall, the Hall of Philosophy, and the Hall of Christ. A walk by the Chautauqua Amphitheater in the afternoon often offers guests the chance to watch a rehearsal for that evening's performance.

Chautauqua's present refreshment building, which is located at Bestor Memorial Plaza, is dignified with the name Refectory, which is a term used for dining rooms in monasteries, boarding schools, or academic institutions. Before the Refectory was opened, guests could get an ice cream cone or a hamburger at a booth located behind the Chautauqua Amphitheater. Notice that the man with the cane is no longer looking at his watch.

44

After refreshments, guests could stroll under the rustic bridge to the back porch of the Chautauqua Amphitheater where the public could (and still can) meet lecturers and performers and possibly walk away with an autograph. Today, this is also where the electronic equipment needed for modern performances is unloaded.

U. S. 417.   The Fountain, Chautauqua Institution.   Chautauqua, N. Y.

This fountain in St. Paul's Grove attracted children just as Bestor Fountain in the plaza does today. Women armed with fans seem to have the children under control. An ornate lantern on a pedestal provided lighting that was different from the usual streetlights.

Alumni Hall was built in 1892 by the alumni of the CLSC. It was to be used for meetings and to display the parade banners created by each year's class. Later, the porch along the building's front was added. It became the location where weekly reviews of CLSC books were held.

Bishop Vincent hoped the Hall of Christ, which was dedicated to the study and worship of Christ, would be the central building on the Chautauqua grounds. Construction commenced in 1900, and the Hall of Christ was dedicated in 1909. Today, it is used for a number of classes, workshops, and lectures, including the annual Archives Heritage Lecture Series. It is also used by the Catholic community for Sunday Mass.

The open-air Hall of Philosophy provided a less formal site for audiences. Many listened from chairs outside the building so that they could come and go as their time permitted without disturbing others. Today, a simulcast of the lecture is offered in the Hall of Christ. The simulcast is a popular alternative on a rainy day.

This postcard shows the approach to the Hall of Philosophy, customarily taken by the CLSC Recognition Day Parade. At times, the steps provide hard seats for overflow audiences at the afternoon lectures.

A walk or, better yet, a bicycle ride past the Hall of Christ, down the brick path, and through the woods leads to Thunder Bridge (so named for the sound a bicycle makes when riding over it). This bridge leads to the south end of the grounds, which was named the Overlook. Pres. Theodore Roosevelt is said to have traveled over this bridge in a carriage during his visit in 1905.

After crossing the bridge, guests would turn left and walk toward the lake. The athletic field was located down the hill on the right. Before the grandstand was erected, spectators sat on the bank overlooking the field. This image shows a game between Youngsville and Chautauqua on August 2, 1906. Some of the women are holding parasols for protection from the sun.

To the left of the field is a ravine with a creek flowing to the lake. These quiet woods provide a wonderful escape into nature. The Bird, Tree, and Garden Club (BGT) has two sites hidden in the woods where they hold lectures on nature and Indian lore.

This building was erected in 1899 for the already-existing Chautauqua Boys' Club, which offered boys a variety of activities such as archery, baseball, tennis, shooting, weight lifting, rowing, gymnastics, and lacrosse.

The Athletic Club made both lake and land sports accessible to adults. There was a bridge from the second floor leading to the athletic field. This building was torn down in 1968 and replaced with the Beeson Youth Center, which is part of the Boys' and Girls' Club complex.

543 The Bathing Beach, Chautauqua, N.Y.

The lakeshore has always been one of Chautauqua's primary attractions. The bathing beach attracted many swimmers, as well as the spectators seen here. It is a wonder that anyone could swim in the heavy woolen suits of the period. As late as the 1950s, rooming houses were required to post a notice that wrappers must be worn over swimsuits on the way to the beach.

This road along the lakeshore is now known as South Lake Drive. Cottages and hotels were situated up the slope and back from this road with a lawn leading down to the lake. This created a parklike setting and provided a change from the dense community in the old section of Chautauqua. The promenade in front of the houses provided picturesque lake views.

This postcard shows the perfect setting for a picnic and then a row on the lake. Boats were available for rent at the nearby dock. Guests would have been able to hear the sound of steamboat whistles as they approached the dock. The Pier Building had bells that chimed out each hour. In addition to the lectures and concerts, Chautauqua gave people a chance to escape the cities for a while.

CHAUTAUQUA, N. Y. Hotel Athenaeum.

Many grand hotels stood along Chautauqua Lake in the 1890s. Even though the Athenaeum Hotel was opened in 1881, it was not completed until 1883. It is the only grand hotel from this period that remains on the lake. Besides providing accommodation and meals during the season, the Athenaeum Hotel is popular for weddings, conferences, and other special events in the spring and fall.

From our Veranda, Chautauqua Institution, Chautauqua, N. Y.

The veranda of the Athenaeum Hotel was a pleasant place to sit in a rocking chair and view the lake. Although the era of steamboats is over, modern-day visitors can still catch a glimpse of the Chautauqua Belle paddling across the lake on excursions from Mayville. This replica of a stern-wheeler steamboat was built in 1975 and is one of the few operating steamboats still in use in the United States.

THE PIER FROM THE ATHENAEUM'S TOWER, CHAUTAUQUA
CHAUTAUQUA, NEW YORK

After 40 years of use, the Athenaeum Hotel's tower had to be removed for safety reasons. However, guests can still to climb to the hotel's dome. This photograph was taken from the tower before it was razed and provides a bird's-eye view of the Pier Building. It was so-named because part of it was constructed on piles in the lake while the other part of the Pier Building was anchored to land.

CHAUTAUQUA, N.Y.   Hotel Lawn, Chautauqua Institution.

This postcard provides a view of the Athenaeum Hotel lawn. Perhaps some event on the lakeshore has just ended and people are leaving for lunch, possibly at the spacious dining room in the Athenaeum Hotel. The men's club can be seen among the trees with its awning-covered upper deck.

The road pictured in this postcard is now paved and the sand pile gone, but there are still benches for guests to sit on and watch the lake. Automobiles are prohibited from driving on South Lake Drive. Today, only bicycles and the South Loop bus share the road with the bicycles and strollers.

The promenade does not have the curving path it once did but it is still a pleasant walk. This scene looks back at the Athenaeum Hotel. For a while, the hotel was painted brown, but people soon grew weary of it and the color was changed to a ivory.

The promenade leads to Miller Park. After a day of lectures and sermons, there were generally fireworks over the lake accompanied by singers and bands that performed on rafts. Later, on the Fourth of July, steamboats on the lake would hold an "Illuminated Fleet" contest in which flares, fireworks, and—eventually—strings of lights were used.

Miller Park is bordered by cottages and by the Arcade Building. Before the construction of the first Chautauqua Amphitheater in 1879, this park was known as the auditorium. It was filled with benches between the trees and set around a camp meeting speaker's stand. Miller Park is where most of the programming of the early Chautauqua assemblies took place.

On the directions of founder, John Vincent, Rev. W.W. Wythe constructed a model of the Holy Land for the first Chautauqua Assembly. It provided a visual teaching aid for the instruction of Sunday school teachers. The model is still used for biblical instruction, and children still enjoy playing there just as Ida Tarbell, a prominent teacher, author, and journalist, did as a girl in her teens.

When the season ended in late August, Chautauqua was at rest. In this postcard, the crowds have left, the docks are on shore, the boats are stored, and the lake is a smooth mirror. The end of the season was a time to slow down and appreciate the beauty of the lake as the leaves changed from green to brilliant fall colors.

In his book *Abaft the Funnel*, Rudyard Kipling remembers a visit to Chautauqua. He writes, "Once inside the grounds on the paths that serpentine round the myriad cottages I was lost in admiration of scores of pretty girls, most of them with little books under their arms and a pretty air of seriousness on their faces."

The lakefront was Chautauqua's front door. Steamboats continually arrived and departed from the large Pier Building. There were shops on the upper floors and on the porches surrounding the Pier Building. A ramp to the second floor from the park made it easy for visitors to wait and watch for friends.

Ten bells were placed in the new Pier Building, constructed in 1886, along with the assembly's new clockworks. Over the years, however, the weight of the clock and bells began causing structural damage and were transferred to the Miller Memorial Bell Tower when it was constructed in 1911.

The Miller Memorial Bell Tower was built in 1911. This Italianate-style tower, designed by E.B. Green, has become the symbol of Chautauqua. The clock, donated by the Seth Thomas Clock Company, continued to keep the official time of Chautauqua for another 50 years. Recently, the clock was restored by John Sirianno and is currently keeping time in the Oliver Archives Center. The Cornell family funded the clock restoration.

By the time the old Pier Building was razed in 1916, the lake was no longer the primary entrance to the grounds. Maintaining the old building became difficult and unnecessary.

The old Pier Building was replaced by this low two-story structure, which was designed to make the bell tower more visible. The building is now home to Chautauqua's College Club. A swimming beach sits just south of the location of the Pier Building.

The North Shore, Assembly, CHAUTAUQUA, N. Y.

Our favorite retreat.

The area north of the bell tower was designated as the North Shore. Rocks were piled along the shoreline at this time to protect against erosion. It was a good place for children to wade and collect clamshells while their parents watched and chatted from the park benches on the shore.

NORTH AVENUE, CHAUTAUQUA INSTITUTION, CHAUTAUQUA, N. Y.

As North Lake Drive leads away from Miller Park, it rises up a slope and bends around to follow the shoreline at a higher elevation. The houses were close to the street, and stairs led down the bluff to the shore. The house at the far right was, at one time, the home of the same Norton family that provided the funds to build Norton Hall.

Four

"Dear Friends: Our Room Here . . ."

In the beginning, a vacation at Chautauqua was really a camping experience. Instead of pitching a tent, guests could, with an annual payment, lease a 40-by-50-foot lot for 99 years and build a simple cottage. These cottages had board walls and joints covered by wood strips (known as board and batten) and were often erected on previous tent platforms. Stud walls were sometimes covered with cloth and then papered. A surprising number of these cottages existed until the 1950s without many improvements.

In the 1880s, many hotels and rooming houses opened on the grounds to accommodate the growing numbers of people coming to Chautauqua. By the early 1900s, most rooming houses served meals. Room and board could cost as much as $10 a week. The rooms had a bed, hanging space for clothes, a dresser, a wall-hung washbowl, and a mirror. The shared bathroom was down the hall. Today, Chautauqua's hotels have been modernized, and most of the rooming houses have been converted to condominiums and apartments.

The Athenaeum Hotel is one of the few resort hotels left on the shores of Chautauqua Lake. Carefully restored to provide modern conveniences, this hotel, with its dining room that seats 300 and an elegant parlor room, provides a glimpse of what it was like to stay at a hotel in the past. The hotel became a temporary White House in October 1996 when Pres. Bill Clinton arrived with his staff to prepare for his debate with Sen. Bob Dole.

THE CARY, CHAUTAUQUA INSTITUTION   CHAUTAUQUA, N. Y.

Like many of Chautauqua's accommodations, the Carey Hotel grew in size from its original mansard-roofed building by gradual additions. At one time, it had a covered walkway over the street to a large annex that is now a separate apartment building. In 1925, George Gershwin stayed at this hotel while visiting Chautauqua to finish his "Concerto in F."

The St. Elmo started in 1890 as a rooming house. It was enlarged by adding on several adjacent houses. Eventually, the whole block was made into a three-story building. Several generations of the same family operated the hotel year-round. This card shows the owners and staff gathered on the different porches of the original building.

Because it was located on the plaza and near many of the buildings that remained open through the year, the St. Elmo was the center of winter activity, and in the summer, it was a natural gathering place for visitors due to its central location. The hotel was eventually torn down and replaced by a condominium building with a restaurant and shops on the lower level.

The Spencer, built around 1907, was located just up the street from the Chautauqua Amphitheater. It had multilevel porches where guests could listen to performances happening in the Chautauqua Amphitheater. At one time, it had an annex across the street. The annex was replaced by condominium apartments around 1980.

The Morey Hotel occupied the space that is now Lincoln Park. The multilevel porches, typical of these hotels, were important in the days before air-conditioning. They provided a good opportunity for guests to get acquainted and talk about their stay at Chautauqua.

THE WINDSOR   THE BELVEDERE   THE LEBANON
LAKE FRONT HOTELS, CHAUTAUQUA INSTITUTION, CHAUTAUQUA, N. Y.

The quiet lakefront hotels offered views, breezes, and spacious front lawns. The Windsor Hotel, seen in this picture, started as the Lafayette in 1881 and was purchased by Nina Wensley in 1952. It was donated to the Chautauqua Institution to serve as a guesthouse for speakers and entertainers. When it was donated, the Windsor Hotel was renamed the Wensley House.

The Belvedere and Golden Rod

The Belvedere and the Goldenrod were joined to the Lebanon to become the Hotel William Baker. The structures in the postcard were replaced with several condominium buildings that could better meet modern codes and expectations. The new building was designed to blend in with the general appearance of the waterfront.

From this postcard, which is postmarked 1916, it appears that the Lebanon has not changed its lower levels, but an extra story and a penthouse with a flat roof have been added. The brick building behind the Lebanon was later removed to allow for further expansion of the hotel.

The Muncie Hotel of 1883 was another lakefront hotel facing North Lake Drive. Like the others, it expanded by adding an annex. In 1944, it became the North Shore Inn. In 1970, it was torn down for a possible new hotel, but a private home was built in its stead.

The Indiana Inn was just north of the Muncie Hotel. It had multiple vine-covered porches that provided a good view of the lake. Whitfield Avenue was directly behind the hotel and provided easy access to Miller Park. The Indiana Inn appears to have been two buildings that were joined. It was torn down in 1937 to make way for a private residence.

The wife of Robert D. Campbell acquired the Indiana Inn and three rooming houses on the opposite side of Whitfield Avenue in 1937. The structures were torn down so that a private residence could be built. The lots across the street were used for a garden and the site of an inconspicuous garage. Henrietta Campbell was active in Chautauqua affairs and became a lifetime trustee.

THE RANSOM, CHAUTAUQUA, N. Y.

The Ransom was located at 9 Whitfield Avenue, across from the site of the North Shore Inn. It had multilevel porches characteristic of Chautauqua. Like many other rooming houses, it was converted to condominium apartments. The new units have kitchens, making the old practice of room and board unnecessary.

THE NEW GLEASON, CHAUTAUQUA INSTITUTION.   CHAUTAUQUA, N. Y.

The Gleason is situated on North Lake Drive overlooking the lake. It still rents rooms, but no longer provides meals. Aside from the various denominational houses, this is one of a few rooming houses remaining on the grounds. Howard Hansen, the composer, stayed at the house pictured on the right when at Chautauqua.

The Aldine is located across from the Athenaeum Hotel. It was built in 1897 and was a popular rooming house. The tower rooms had a great view of the lake. Theodore Roosevelt is said to have stayed here on one of his four visits. The Aldine has followed the trend and is now a condominium.

The Colonnade Cottage is another rooming house that has been converted to a condominium. This postcard from 1912 shows that it enjoyed a wonderful view of the lake.

The Albion on South Terrace, with its mansard roof similar to the Colonnade Cottage, was built around 1885. The slope of the land towards the lake enabled these buildings to have four usable stories on the lakeside. This longtime rooming house now has condominium apartments.

The Keystone was another rooming house composed of two joined buildings. Its location on Roberts Avenue adjacent to the Chautauqua Amphitheater made it possible to see the programs from the hotel's second-floor porch. It has been converted into a luxury condominium complete with elevator service.

The Longfellow, built in 1883, was another mansard-roofed boardinghouse. This roof style allowed the upper floor rooms to have adequate ceiling height with dormers to provide for windows. The building had an addition placed on the rear lot in 1885. This, too, was remodeled to become a condominium.

The Arlington, on the corner of Roberts and Vincent Avenues, shows the style of the 1890s with its ornate porch scrolls. It sat on one-and-a-half lots and had a very small cottage adjacent to it on the half lot. It is presumed that those posing in front are the owners and staff. This building is also now a condominium.

The Columbia consisted of three adjacent buildings in 1903: two on Roberts Avenue next to the Chautauqua Amphitheater and one on South Terrace Avenue (pictured here). These were acquired by the Ministers Union in 1930. The Westervelt on South Terrace Avenue was added to the Ministers Union's holdings in 1990. Now called the Ecumenical Community of Chautauqua, this facility offers a rooming house experience with a communal kitchen at reasonable rates.

The New Wesley at 51 North Terrace Avenue was located on the corner of North Terrace and Hedding Avenues. Hedding Avenue is now Vincent Avenue as it goes toward the lake from Bestor Plaza. The New Wesley was torn down to make way for the Miller Cottage garden. The Miller Cottage can be seen in the background of this card.

The Ohio Cottage at 18 Morris Avenue was built in 1895 and became the Talley-Ho Restaurant in 1942. It has operated as a popular restaurant since then. The Talley-Ho also has rental rooms and apartments. The property extends from Morris Avenue to North Terrace Avenue.

The Chadakoin operated for many years as a rooming house at 24 Peck Avenue. It was sold in 1956 and is now the Episcopal House. It and other denominational houses line the brick walk also known as Clark Street. The Episcopal House provides rooms at reasonable rates for visiting clergy and others as space allows.

THE ASHLAND
~~RATES $7.00 TO $12.00~~

MRS. DELIGHT DAVIS DONNEL
CHAUTAUQUA N.Y

The Ashland on Vincent Avenue near the post office was built in 1902. In this postcard, the Ashland advertises room and board rates that range from $7 to $12. It is now a condominium with apartments to rent. From 1980 to the present has seen most of the old rooming houses have been converted to condominiums with modern conveniences and facilities such as private kitchens and bathrooms. Many of these condominium apartments are rented by the week in summer and winterized for use in the off-season.

The Glen Park Cottage had a view of the plaza from its location on Morris Avenue. It was a large rooming house in the 1800s. In this picture, the architecture is somewhat mixed in style as shown by the stick-built decorations of the porch posts, which contrast with the shingled sidewalls. These multilevel porches were a necessity in summer.

Extensions were added to the right side of the Glen Park Cottage and included an enclosed first-floor porch and a dormer on the roof to make the fourth floor usable. This card, postmarked in 1928, shows that the place had become a cafeteria with rooms above to rent. It was a popular eating place until 1982 when it was torn down to make way for the Glen Park Condominium.

The Food Shoppe was a small eating place run by a room and board establishment on Miller Avenue. It continued as a boardinghouse until the 1980s when it was converted to condominium apartments. Its location a block away from the plaza and the library made it a convenient place to stay.

The Hearthstone Lodge at 11 Ramble Avenue looked more like a residence with its bungalow-style shingles and dormer. The casement windows with diamond panes are an unusual feature—most houses were still using double-hung windows at the time. The gable dormer with its circular attic window is also different in style.

Five

"DEAR FRIENDS: WE WENT TO CHURCH . . ."

Although primarily organized by Methodists at the start, Chautauqua has always been ecumenical. All mainstream Protestant churches took part in the first assembly in 1874 and have since been joined by other Christians and those of other faiths. Vincent encouraged denominations to build their own houses of worship and to provide accommodation for ministers and others associated with their church.

The Chautauqua program has always included a communal morning service and eventide on Sundays. Services were first held in the auditorium (now Miller Park) and later in the Chautauqua Amphitheater. Each week, the morning service provided the opportunity for guests to hear renowned ministers from different churches. Even today, this draws in many people from the area as well as those who are staying on the grounds. For many years, the gates were closed on Sundays and people could neither enter nor leave the grounds unless they had special permission. Today, the gates are open on Sundays and admission to the grounds is free.

Sunday morning fills the Chautauqua Amphitheater with worshipers as they come to hear ministers from different denominations. Guests must have felt a special serenity when attending those summer-morning services. The place was open to the breeze blowing through the surrounding trees and sheltered guests from the noises of modern life.

THE SERVICE OF APPROACH TO THE HALL OF CHRIST
CHAUTAUQUA INSTITUTION, CHAUTAUQUA, NEW YORK.

This was the service of the dedication of the Hall of Christ with Bishop John Vincent at the lectern. This building was Bishop Vincent's dream of an impressive structure that showed Chautauqua's dedication to faith.

Hurlbut Memorial Church was built in 1931 as a Methodist community church open to all faiths. Since 1960, the church has been used for Jewish services during the season. The regular congregation serves lunches and some dinners during the summer to raise money for their mission and serve the public need.

The Methodist House, directly across from the Chautauqua Amphitheater, was built in 1887. The original chapel at the rear was replaced in the early 1950s. More recently, a second story was added to provide more housing for guests.

The Hall of Missions, alongside the Hall of Philosophy, the Hall of Christ, and Alumni Hall, encircle St. Paul's Grove. The Hall of Missions was built in 1924 to serve as headquarters for Chautauqua's Department of Religion. Various groups used it for services and meeting, and the porch provided a pleasant space for discussion.

CHAPEL OF THE GOOD SHEPHERD *(Episcopal)*, CHAUTAUQUA, NEW YORK

The Chapel of the Good Shepherd was built in 1894. It is adjacent to the Hall of Christ. The projecting hood in this type of architecture was meant to house a bell. The interior of this small chapel has seating for 150 people and is used for services during the season. During the off-season, it is popular for weddings. Although an Episcopalian chapel, Roman Catholics use the chapel today for daily Masses.

The United Methodist Missionary Home is located at 34 South Lake Drive. It provides housing and meals for vacationing missionaries and others as space allows. Constructed in 1903, it replaced an ornate cottage built for the daughter of Clement Studebaker. A major contributor to Chautauqua, Clement Studebaker served briefly as president of Chautauqua after the death of Lewis Miller.

The Fenton Memorial Deaconess Home was built by the Methodist Episcopal Church as a residence for deaconesses at Chautauqua. Its formal columned porches and rectangular profile caused it to stand out from the surrounding summer homes. It is still located on the corner of Wythe and Hawthorne Avenues in the Overlook.

The Congregational House faces the Chautauqua Amphitheater on Bowman Avenue. The Congregational Church established a denominational house on this land in 1882 and took over an adjacent house in 1914. These buildings were torn down to construct this neoclassical brick building in 1931. It became the United Church of Christ building in 1964.

This small chapel was located at 28 Vincent Avenue. It was used by the Presbyterian Church from about 1889 until 1958 when the St. Elmo purchased it and remodeled it for a guest cottage. It was torn down in 1985 when the hotel was razed to make way for the St. Elmo Condominium complex.

The Presbyterian Headquarters was opened in 1890. Located at 9 Palestine Avenue, it is on the south side of the Chautauqua Amphitheater. This early view from around 1914 shows that the annex at the rear of the building was in place to provide additional housing.

This view of the Presbyterian Headquarters is probably from the 1920s. The wooden porch has been replaced by masonry and is now a two-story porch with metal railings. Programs on the Chautauqua Amphitheater stage could be enjoyed while sitting on these porches. A recent brick addition to the lakeside of the Presbyterian Headquarters doubled the available accommodations.

HEADQUARTERS OF THE DISCIPLES OF CHRIST, CHAUTAUQUA INSTITUTION, CHAUTAUQUA, N. Y.

The headquarters of the Disciples of Christ at 32 Clark Street (the brick walk shown in the postcard) was built in 1896. Its imposing porch must have been added at a later date, as its style is not consistent with the typical mansard roofing. There is another structure that provides additional rooms located on Janes Avenue behind the headquarters building.

BAPTIST HEADQUARTERS, CHAUTAUQUA INSTITUTION, CHAUTAUQUA, N.Y.

The Baptist headquarters was built in 1894. It faces the brick walk at 35 Clark Street. Like many of the Chautauqua buildings of that period, it has the semblance of a Queen Anne–style tower. The striped awnings must have shut out much of the daylight in the upper room.

Located at the corner of Pratt and Center Avenues, the Episcopal Cottage faced the plaza. It may have been a rooming house until it was bought by the Episcopal Church in 1918. There appear to have been changes made to the building, as the third floor with its flat roof seems out of character. It was sold in 1956 and razed and replaced by a private residence in 1964.

The Lutheran House was built in 1925. It stands on the corner of Peck Avenue and Clark Street. Its architecture is unique with its reddish-brown brick and arched porch. So that they would last longer, a number of the denominational houses were constructed of masonry—a contrast to the large wooden structures of the older church houses.

Located on the corner of Miller and Pratt Avenues, this rooming house was known as the Salem. The rates for room and board ranged from $6 to $8 a week in 1901. It became the Reformed Church House in 1924, and after the merger with the Congregational Church, it became the house of the United Church of Christ.

Built in 1889, this Queen Anne–style house on the corner of Clark Street and Cookman Avenue served as the Unitarian Universalist House. It was purchased in 1904 and sold as a private residence in 1963. The porches overlook the Hall of Philosophy. One of the torches of the Hall of Philosophy can be seen in foreground to the right. Today, there is a new Unitarian House.

Six

"DEAR FRIENDS: TODAY WE LEARNED . . ."

From its inception, Chautauqua has been a place to learn while vacationing in a natural setting. There was a growing desire for higher education among Americans of the 19th century, but it would not be until well into the 20th century that most could attend high school, let alone college. Even libraries were few and far between. Chautauqua, more than any other American institution, addressed this problem by reaching out to all Americans regardless of their age, sex, religion, or race.

In addition to the classes offered at Chautauqua in the summer, John Vincent initiated a four-year correspondence reading course in 1878 named the Chautauqua Literary and Scientific Circle, or simply the CLSC. Its purpose was to provide those who were too poor, too busy, or lived too far away to attend college the opportunity to receive the equivalent of a college education by reading in their spare time throughout the year. After completing the course, graduates were encouraged to come to Chautauqua to receive their certificates of recognition and participate in the Recognition Day ceremonies.

The School of Languages was formed in 1879 at Chautauqua and was followed by a teachers' retreat and the School of Theology. These and other efforts led to the chartering of Chautauqua University, which existed from 1883 until 1892. After the university closed, Chautauqua continued to offer opportunities to study music, art, theater, writing, and religion.

While only a few thousand students could attend the Chautauqua Institution during a given summer, hundreds of thousands more could be reached by teaching teachers. Regular features of Chautauqua training included hands-on learning, standardized curriculum, normal school training, and graduated classes. It was at Chautauqua that William Sherwood taught his system of musical training to teachers. Chautauqua was one of the first institutions where teachers could learn the manual and fine arts and where coaches could be certified. Chautauqua also had one of the first photography schools. It was a pioneer in preschool education and in formal training and certification for kindergarten teachers.

CHAUTAUQUA, N. Y. College Hall.

This building was the home of the Chautauqua University. It was built in 1887 at College Hill Park. It was nicknamed the "The Moorish Barn" due to the elaborate porticos and domes. The building was razed to make room for the Arts and Crafts Building.

SCHOOL OF PEDAGOGY

The training of teachers has long been part of Chautauqua. The Hall of Pedagogy is now known by the more mundane name, the Hall of Education. It was built on College Hill in 1898 and moved south of the present Arts and Crafts Building in 1911.

Sherwood Memorial Studio (built in 1912) is named after William Sherwood (1854–1911), a revered piano maestro and teacher. This building resembles the look of the Arts and Crafts Building with the columns and brown-shingle sidewalls. It was recently renovated and remains a building for music instruction.

"Practice Shacks" were built over many years. By 1922, there were 39 practice buildings, one office, and five other studios. Recently, some have been moved to make room for the new music buildings. The Practice Shacks have since been renovated with air-conditioning.

A variety of subjects have been taught in the Chautauqua summer schools, including gardening, as is seen in this postcard from 1912. During World War I, the Women's Land Army planted Victory Gardens at Chautauqua to support the war effort. Chautauqua has recently set aside small plots by Bryant Avenue to enable individuals to have vegetable gardens.

This is an elementary school known as the Children's School, built in 1921. Families coming to Chautauqua can still enroll their children in a development-based morning preschool program. A bus picks up the children and brings them back to convenient drop-off points.

A KINDERGARTEN GROUP.
CHAUTAUQUA INSTITUTION, CHAUTAUQUA, NEW YORK.

This picture of two teachers and kindergartners with various playthings was taken on the plaza. John Dewey from the University of Chicago was the kindergarten supervisor in the early 1900s. The sign on the boardinghouse in the background designates it as "The Roberts," which was located at the corner of Center and Pratt Avenues.

The Flower Girls - Recognition Day.
Chautauqua Institution, Chautauqua, New York.

Children participated in various functions at Chautauqua, including Children's Day, Old First Night, and as flower girls for the CLSC Recognition Day. They are lined up here in 1900 with their parents in the background. The Children's Temple, which can be seen behind them, was given to the institution by Lewis Miller in 1878. It stood in the plaza across from the present Smith Memorial Library.

Here, flower girls are preparing for the CLSC Recognition Day ceremony. They strewed flowers in front of the graduating class as they proceeded from the Golden Gate to the Hall of Philosophy. Some look as though they were not so happy to be a part of the event.

This picture of an outdoor children's class was taken near the Arts and Crafts Quadrangle. The lodge can be seen in the background. The Children's School provided training for the teachers as well as the students.

ARTS AND CRAFTS SCHOOL, CHAUTAUQUA, CHAUTAUQUA, N. Y.

The first section of the Arts and Crafts Quadrangle was built in 1909, with the wings added at later dates. It provides studios for instruction in fabric arts, ceramics, sculpture, jewelry, and painting. Recently, a state-of-the-art kiln has been added behind the building.

Summer School Dormitory   Chautauqua, N. Y.

The Lincoln Dormitory was built in 1912 as an infirmary and, shortly after, became a staff residence. The Jackson-Carnahan Dance Studios, home of the School of Dance under Jean-Pierre Bonnefoux, stand nearby on Palestine and Hedding Avenues.

Kellogg Hall. Chautauqua Institution, Chautauqua, New York.

Kellogg Hall was erected in 1889 on what is now Bestor Memorial Plaza. In 1905, it was moved to its present location. Kellogg Hall has served as the Women's Christian Temperance Union (WCTU) headquarters, housed classrooms, the registrar's offices, and the offices of the *Chautauquan Daily*. It was thoroughly renovated in 2009 and is now a visual arts complex with exhibition space.

Higgins Hall, built in 1895, has also been used for classes, exhibits, and motion pictures. It is now known as the Cinema Theater and shows a variety of selected movies. The inside of the cinema still has hammer-beam trusses that retain a sense of the original interior.

Seven

"Dear Friends: Today We Had Fun . . ."

Recreation has been one of the four essential elements, or pillars, of the Chautauqua program, along with religion, education, and art, and a key attraction since the first assembly in 1874. People have always taken time from their busy Chautauqua schedule to enjoy what the lake had to offer, take a walk in the woods, or play a game of croquet. Bishop Vincent had tennis courts built at Chautauqua after being introduced to the game on a trip to England. Chautauqua soon provided the facilities for many sports and instruction on how to play them. College students and coaches promoted many of the sports they enjoyed at their various schools, including baseball, football, gymnastics, and rowing. Group pictures showed players wearing their jerseys from schools such as Harvard or Yale.

This postcard shows people gathering along the lakeshore near the Pier Building perhaps to watch a pageant. Besides being the main means of transportation, steamboats provided special entertainment with an illuminated fleet contest and fireworks on the Fourth of July.

The Men's Club at the end of Palestine Park was built to look like a small castle. In this postcard, the awning-covered roof terrace provides a place for the band to play while the audience strolled about to listen to the concert. Band concerts are still a regular feature of the program at Chautauqua.

This scene from the late 1930s shows the Chautauqua Sports Club, formerly the Men's Club. It was originally designed as a power plant. Today, the Men's Club meets in the Women's Clubhouse and men can join the Women's Club if they wish.

Shuffleboard is still a popular game at Chautauqua and the courts stay busy. The women's dresses were long in the 1930s compared to today, but not as long as they were in the early 1900s. These courts were replaced when the Sports Club was built to replace the Men's Club.

The new sports club building was constructed in 1942. It provided facilities for shuffleboard, horseshoes, lawn bowling, bridge, and other games. It has docking facilities with rental paddleboats, kayaks, and canoes. It is the starting point for the annual Chautauqua Old First Night Run, which is a 2.7-mile race through the grounds.

Chautauqua has a group devoted to bowling on this green. Throwing the balls requires considerable skill by the bowler because they curve as they roll down the carefully clipped green.

The Chautauqua Roque Club, Chautauqua Institution. Chautauqua, New York.

Roque is no longer played at Chautauqua. It was played on a croquet-like court with cement curbs on all four sides. Although it uses mallets and wickets similar to those used in croquet, the ball may be ricocheted off the curbs as well. The courts were located in the ravine near the Girls' Club. It is possible to find some fragments of the curbs remaining there.

The Boys' Club is on the lakefront at the foot of Hawthorne Avenue. Built in 1899, it has served many generations of young Chautauquans through the years. Notice the bicycles leaning against the building. Today, the club buildings are surrounded by hundreds of bicycles belonging to young people who use them to go back and forth from the club.

A 2814 b. The Chautauqua Boys' Club, Assembly Grounds Chautauqua Lake, N. Y. 1904

CHAUTAUQUA, N. Y.
Girl's Club, Chautauqua Institution.
5675

The Girls' Club (built in 1902) is located on the far side of South Lake Drive, across from the other club buildings. It was recently remodeled extensively, although the exterior looks the same. The present-day Boys' and Girls' Clubs offer an extensive day camp program for youth aged seven to 17 years old. There are generations who return to Chautauqua because of the program and the friendships they made.

AT THE "GYM".
CHAUTAUQUA INSTITUTION, CHAUTAUQUA, NEW YORK.

This postcard, which is postmarked 1910, shows the children and adults who participated in the club programs posing for a photograph in front of the gymnasium built in 1890. It also served as the School of Physical Education, which offered the country's first certificates in physical education.

This is a view of the students of the School of Physical Education, which offered a six-week training course for physical education teachers led by Dr. Jay Seaver, a professor at Yale. This photograph, taken around 1907, shows Seaver standing with hat in hand on the far right.

There was a bathing beach just north of the Pier Building. This postcard shows children wading and playing among the rocks that lined the shore as a break wall. There appears to be a boathouse shed at the dock beyond the beach.

The Bathing Girl at Chautauqua,
Chautauqua Institution, Chautauqua, N. Y.

This pensively posed girl wearing the bulky bathing suit and black stockings might well be considering whether it is worth getting wet or whether she should find someone to take her out in a rowboat. Rowboats like the one pictured were often pointed on both ends and designed to be easy to row.

At the Bathing Beach,
Chautauqua Institution, Chautauqua, N. Y.

This bathing scene shows a variety of attire, from women wading in their skirts and stockings to men on the dock with jackets and ties. The couple and the child at the far left are posed like dolls in their fancy street clothes.

This is a swimming scene from a later date than the previous postcard. The women in the white dresses are probably mothers watching over their children, while the girl standing in a half-crouching position is either considering a dive or is uncomfortably wet, weighed down by her bathing costume.

The diving platform proved to be a popular addition to the swimming area. Two platforms and two boards were set at gradual levels to accommodate divers with greater or less skill and nerve.

The institution provided these sleek double-ender rowboats for rent. The Golding and the Lebanon appear in the background. On the far right, a woman can be seen approaching the sulfur spring adjacent to the Men's Club.

Many of the postcards sent to friends mention fathers and sons fishing every day. The most prized catch was the muskellunge, which was often caught by trolling. Lines were tied to each leg so the fisherman could feel a strike while he rowed. The catch pictured in this postcard, a good-sized muskellunge, is at first hard to detect because it is aligned with the fisherman's leg.

A 2831 Pier House and Lake, Chautauqua.   Aug. 19, 1905

My Dear Hazel: I will send you a picture of Chautauqua Leak. I hope you and the kittens are having a good time. Your friend 35 James av Fred A Mill

Before March 1907, post office regulations did not allow anything on the back of cards but the address. Out of necessity, any message was short and often written on the picture. In this case, the card allowed some space for writing on the front. Steamboats were always coming and going from the pier, as was the case in this photograph.

THE CHAUTAUQUA BOAT CREW. CHAUTAUQUA INSTITUTION, CHAUTAUQUA, NEW YORK.

There was competition between the Chautauqua Boat Crew and the Chadakoin Rowing Crew, which became the Lakewood Yacht Club after rowing ceased to be a popular sport on the lake. The Chautauqua Boat Crew trained out of the Athletic Club. Some training was also made available to Boys' Club members at that time.

The Miller Memorial Bell Tower has been the iconic symbol for Chautauqua since it was built in 1911. This serene view of a sailboat passing by the tower as it approaches the dock suggests that sailing was a perfect way to enjoy the lake.

The Chautauqua Yacht Club has been an active group over many years and has sailed with many classes of boats as they developed. The lake, with its surrounding hills, presents some challenges for sailing because the gusts of wind are variable and storms can be unpredictable.

Because it was located next to the ball field, the tennis courts, and the lake, the Athletic Club was the center for sports both on and off the water. This view of the docks from 1916 shows an early speedboat, which is thought to be the Phoenix. Even though it only had a four-cylinder gasoline engine, the Phoenix was the fastest boat on the lake at that time.

The era of the private steam launch eventually gave way to the motorboat. This early speedboat preceded the varnished mahogany Chris-Craft and Century boats of the 1930s and 1940s. The people in this craft must have considered boating a formal activity. The yachting caps, jackets, and pennants indicate the pride of owning such a fast boat.

Baseball was a major spectator sport at Chautauqua. This panoramic picture from about 1909 shows the crowd of spectators that assembled to watch a game. In 1912, a grandstand was built to replace the backstop shown here. The bridge can be seen leading off the field to the second story of the Athletic Club. The tennis courts are on the far right. Sports received

The Athletic Field, Chautauqua Institution, Chautauqua, N. Y

an early boost when William Raney Harper, a Yale professor and head of the Chautauqua University, convinced Amos Alonzo Stagg, one of Yale's top athletes, to come to Chautauqua with some of his athletic classmates. Stagg returned to Chautauqua for many years as speaker in the Chautauqua Amphitheater.

Tennis was introduced to Chautauqua by John Vincent, who had courts built after encountering the game in England. The evolution of the game to lawn tennis came with the invention of a vulcanized ball that would not destroy the grass court. Soon, clay surfaces became the most popular type of playing courts in this country.

The first golf course at Chautauqua was laid out behind the college buildings in 1896. Professional Lake Placid golfers laid out a nine-hole course across the highway in 1913. In 1924, Donald Ross redesigned the course to expand it to 18 holes. The clubhouse seen in this picture burned in 1976 and was replaced in 1977.

GOLFING, CHAUTAUQUA INSTITUTION, CHAUTAUQUA, NEW YORK

This tournament from around 1916 appears to have preceded the fashion of plus fours for men, although the man on the right may be wearing them. Notice that the women among the spectators are walking the course in skirts that brush the ground.

Sixth Hole and Water Hazard on Golf Course
Chautauqua Institution, Chautauqua, N. Y.
1914

Although this scene at the water hazard is marked 1914 on the card, it appears to be of a later date. For many years, the view of the course from the highway was of two buckets on a ladder-like stand at each hole with no trees to break up the expanse of grass.

Activity at Chautauqua continued well past the summer. A number of year-round residents enjoyed the abundant snow. Bobsledding on the streets to the lake was fun since the weight of all those riders could give the sled extra speed. Streets in Chautauqua are kept open in winter, but just enough snow is left so that sledding and cross–country skiing are possible.

At times the lake freezes without a heavy covering of snow. This is the time for ice boating. Here an ice boat is seen in front of the old Pier Building. This photograph can be dated within a few years, as the Bell Tower was built in 1911 and the Pier Building was torn down in 1916. Now, iceboats have given way to snowmobiles as a way to speed over the frozen lake.

Eight

"DEAR FRIENDS: WE JOINED . . ."

There is always plenty to do at Chautauqua. Keeping informed of the many events and programs offered makes the daily newspaper a necessity. The *Chautauquan Daily* comes out six days a week in the summer and can be bought on the street or in the bookstore. Chautauqua has always encouraged people to become involved and there are many groups to join. Chautauqua has groups that support the opera, theater, dance, symphony, arts, religious discussions, conservation, and other endeavors. Some groups develop programs of their own and bring in outside experts and speakers, while others invite Chautauquans to contribute their skills by performing in the band, reviewing a book or work of music, or by teaching a class.

Chautauqua Woman's Club House, Chautauqua Institution
Chautauqua, N. Y.

The Chautauqua Women's Club first met at the elaborate Victorian home of Jacob Miller and his wife. Located on the site of the present building that overlooks the lake, the Miller home was designed by F.J. and W.A. Kidd of Buffalo and constructed in 1929. Eleanor Roosevelt was a close friend of Anna Hardwicke Pennybacker (1861–1938), president of the Chautauqua Women's Club from 1917 to 1938. Eleanor Roosevelt made several visits to Chautauqua between 1927 and 1937. She spoke in the Chautauqua Amphitheater and at the Hall of Philosophy, and she was interviewed on local radio. She was made a life member after she hosted the Women's Club in Albany, New York, while her husband was serving as New York's governor. She later invited the entire Women's Club to the White House.

The Golden Gate is part of the elaborate Recognition Day ceremony for the CLSC. The path passing through the gate leads to the Hall of Philosophy. No one is allowed to pass through the gate unless the official known as the "Keeper of the Keys" is assured that they have completed the requirements for graduation.

During the Recognition Day ceremony, the graduating class would proceed up the path leading to the Hall of Philosophy. The special procession included festooned arches and girls strewing flowers at the graduates' feet as they walked. They would have attended a candle-lit vigil in the Hall of Philosophy the night before in preparation for the Recognition Day ceremony.

This ceremony is still conducted today by the CLSC. Anyone who wishes to join only needs to sign up and read the required books. After completing the books, they and their classmates are honored with a procession and ceremony. Each class creates a banner to be carried at the Recognition Day parade. Classes continue to meet each year to become reacquainted and work together on projects of their choice.

This is the parade of the banners on Recognition Day. Each graduating class makes a banner and chooses a motto. A few years ago, the Smithsonian Institution displayed many of these banners in an exhibit on Chautauqua. The banners are under the care of the Alumni Association. The older retired banners are stored in the Oliver Archives Center.

Bishop John Vincent, cofounder of Chautauqua, returned to take part in this Recognition Day ceremony (he is in the middle of the three men at center in the photograph). In 1878, his initiation of the four-year reading course now known as the CLSC started a national cultural movement.

The Grange building at 8 Simpson Avenue was constructed in 1908. Lewis Miller was a strong supporter of this national farmers' cooperative movement. Its founder, Oliver Hudson Kelley, organized the first Grange in nearby Fredonia, New York. Grange Day was celebrated at Chautauqua each August 3. Farmers and their families met at the Grange building and spent the day attending special Chautauqua programs.

FRANCES WILLARD HOUSE, CHAUTAUQUA INSTITUTION   CHAUTAUQUA, N. Y.

Chautauqua was all about and all for temperance. A national Woman's Christian Temperance Union (WCTU) convention was organized in the auditorium (now Miller Park) at the first Chautauqua Assembly in 1874. Many famous temperance speakers came to Chautauqua, including Frances E. Willard. This Carpenter Gothic house (1883) at 32 South Lake Avenue, now a private residence, was the headquarters for the WCTU from 1925.

The YMCA and YWCA worked closely with Chautauqua both in New York and on the circuits. This building was the YWCA Hospitality House, which was owned by the national YWCA from 1919 until 1965, when Helen Logan purchased it and donated it to the Chautauqua Institution. Since then, it has been known as the Logan Dormitory. Today, the large first floor is used as the offices for the *Chautauqua Daily*.

Staff, 6th N. S. S. Camp, Chautauqua Institution, Chautauqua, N. Y.

Patriotism was strong during World War I, and women were not to be left out. A woman at Chautauqua in 1918 may have joined the National Service School. During this time, George Vincent's wife, Louise, acted as commandant of the school. Classes were held in food conservation, first aid, dietetics, telegraphy, surgical dressings, typewriting, and Braille.

Building Tool House, 6th N. S. S. Camp, Chautauqua Institution, Chautauqua, N. Y.

This postcard shows a change from the Victorian lady who was often supposed to be frail and in need of protection. In the era leading up to women's suffrage, women insisted on having more serious training to support the war effort. Some of the women who were trained at Chautauqua went on to serve overseas. Given the fencing in place, this photograph may have been taken on the south end of the grounds at the Overlook.

The Drill, Chautauqua Institution, Chautauqua, N. Y.

Reveille was at 6:00 a.m. and taps at 10:00 p.m. This drill in the plaza seems to be a formal occasion with all the Service Corps members, except for the commanding officer, dressed in white.

Smith-Wilkes Hall was built for Chautauqua's Bird, Tree, and Garden Club (BTG), which was also affectionately known as the "Twigs and Tweeters Club." Today, it remains one of the most important independent organizations at Chautauqua. It started as part of the conservation movement and has done much to enhance and protect the natural setting of the Chautauqua grounds. Lectures on related topics are given both at the hall and in the natural settings of the ravine.

Nine

"Dear Friends: Chautauqua at Home . . ."

It was not the intention of the founders that Chautauqua should simply be a summer event. What mattered most was what people carried away with them when they left. This was how Chautauqua made a real difference in the world. Many who visited Chautauqua wished to create their own Chautauqua closer to home. But people still wanted to be connected. At first, the *Chautauquan* magazine, the primary source of required reading for the CLSC program, kept people informed about what was going on at Chautauqua. This was later supplemented by the *Chautauqua Weekly*. Many people who could not attend in the summer or who could attend for only part of the season would subscribe to the *Chautauquan Daily*. Having the periodical mailed to their homes ensured they could stay in touch with what was happening at Chautauqua.

Today, Chautauqua is accessible all year on the Internet at www.ciweb.org. From the website, those interested in Chautauqua can sign up to receive its e-newsletter, listen to podcasts of previous events, and take part in online seminars. There are also Chautauqua events and symposia held at Chautauqua and elsewhere during the off-season. Daughter Chautauquas are still in existence, including some that have recently been revived. They can be found throughout the United States and Canada. Daughter Chautauquas stay in touch with each other through the Chautauqua Network, which was created by the late Chautauqua Institution historian, Alfreda Irwin (1913–2000).

15257. Boulder Colorado Chautauqua Auditorium. Flatirons in Background

The Colorado Chautauqua Association in Boulder continues to thrive and carry out the ideas that inspired the associated Chautauquas. It was founded in 1898 and is the only Chautauqua that has remained in continuous operation west of the Mississippi.

Band Stand, Forest Park, Shelbyville, Ill., Chautauqua

Shelbyville is a town in central Illinois. The Chautauqua building was constructed in 1903 to house related programs. Today, it is used for events and the annual Chautauqua celebration. The scene in this postcard, located at nearby Forest Park, may have been a circuit Chautauqua. A tent similar to those used by traveling Chautauquas can be seen at the right.

122

52153 C. L. S. C Building, Chautauqua Grounds, Mt. Gretna, Pa.

Mount Gretna is located east of Harrisburg, Pennsylvania. In 1892, the United Brethren Church and the Pennsylvania Chautauqua began holding programs at the mountain. The Mount Gretna Chautauqua evolved from using camp meeting tents to Victorian cottages much like other Chautauquas did. It is part of the Chautauqua Network and has summer programs.

52158 Camp Meeting Auditorium, Mt. Gretna, Pa.

The auditorium at Mount Gretna was built in 1899. It is interesting that not just the programs but also the facilities, such as the Chautauqua Amphitheater and the Hall of Philosophy, were copied at daughter Chautauquas. Even a lake was considered essential and most new Chautauquas were built on lakes. If no lake was available, one was sometimes created to reproduce the Chautauqua experience.

123

Cedar Point is an amusement park near Sandusky, Ohio, and next to the Lakeside Chautauqua. This is a Chautauqua gathering from the early 1900s. The Lakeside Chautauqua, once known as the Chautauqua of the Great Lakes, is on a nearby peninsula. Lakeside continues to operate a summer-season program and is an active member of the Chautauqua Network.

Farmington, Iowa, had a Chautauqua Assembly that started in 1904. The Daisy Circle pictured in this postcard was probably a CLSC circle. A program flier from 1909 shows that they hosted circuit Chautauquas for 10 days each summer.

In many towns of rural America, the CLSC circles, the local Chautauquas, and the traveling Chautauquas were the only venues for culture and entertainment. This assembly in Richmond, Indiana, existed for 20 years until 1923.

Chautauqua was often the major event of the summer for a small town in America. Town committees would work to raise the necessary advance money, usually by selling shares, and arrange for the space needed to host the event.

This is a postcard of a travelling Chautauqua. Traveling Chautauquas did not typically arrive en masse like a circus. Speakers and entertainers would perform in one place and then board a train to perform at the next stop on the circuit, as the speakers and entertainers for the following day were arriving.

In time, differences over religion, politics, and social issues divided the Chautauquas. The tent Chautauquas of the 1920s were often ridiculed in the press as being uncultured and out-of-date. This characterization did not mesh with the more sophisticated and upscale image that some Chautauquas were interested in portraying during the 20th century. By 1933, traveling Chautauquas had disappeared in the United States, but they continued in Canada until World War II.

BIBLIOGRAPHY

Cram, Mary Francis Bestor. *Chautauqua Salute: A Memoir of the Bestor Years*. Chautauqua, NY: Chautauqua Institution, 1990.

Crocker, Kathleen, and Jane Currie. *Chautauqua Institution, 1874–1974*. Charleston, SC: Arcadia Publishing, 2001.

Hurlbut, Jesse L. *The Story of Chautauqua*. New York: G.P. Putnam's Sons, 1921.

Irwin, Alfreda L. *Three Taps of the Gavel: Pledge to the Future*. Chautauqua, NY: Chautauqua Institution, 1987.

Levin, Dorothy E., and Karen E. Livsey. *Along Chautauqua Lake*. Charleston, SC: Arcadia Publishing, 2010.

Morrison, Theodore. *Chautauqua: A Center for Education, Religion, and the Arts in America*. Chicago, IL: The University of Chicago Press, 1974.

Simpson, Jeffrey. *Chautauqua: An American Utopia*. New York: Harry N. Abrams, Inc., in association with the Chautauqua Institution, 1999.

Rieser, Andrew C. *The Chautauqua Moment: Protestants, Progressives, and the Culture of Modern Liberalism*. New York: Columbia University Press, 2003.

Vincent, John H. *The Chautauqua Movement*. Boston: Chautauqua Press, 1886.

Warren, R.M. *Chautauqua Sketches: Fair Point and the Sunday-School Assembly*: Descriptive History. Buffalo, NY: H.H. Otis, 1878.

www.arcadiapublishing.com

Discover books about the town where you grew up, the cities where your friends and families live, the town where your parents met, or even that retirement spot you've been dreaming about. Our Web site provides history lovers with exclusive deals, advanced notification about new titles, e-mail alerts of author events, and much more.

MADE IN THE USA

Arcadia Publishing, the leading local history publisher in the United States, is committed to making history accessible and meaningful through publishing books that celebrate and preserve the heritage of America's people and places. Consistent with our mission to preserve history on a local level, this book was printed in South Carolina on American-made paper and manufactured entirely in the United States.

This book carries the accredited Forest Stewardship Council (FSC) label and is printed on 100 percent FSC-certified paper. Products carrying the FSC label are independently certified to assure consumers that they come from forests that are managed to meet the social, economic, and ecological needs of present and future generations.

FSC
Mixed Sources
Product group from well-managed
forests and other controlled sources

Cert no. SW-COC-001530
www.fsc.org
© 1996 Forest Stewardship Council

Find Your Place in History.